SOLVE IT WITH SCIENCE

ROBBERIES AND HEISTS

JOHN TOWNSEND

A⁺

Smart Apple Media

This book has been published in cooperation with Arcturus Publishing Limited.

Series concept: Alex Woolf
Editor and picture researcher: Alex Woolf
Designer: Tall Tree

Published in the United States by Smart Apple Media
P.O. Box 3263, Mankato, Minnesota 56002

Printed in China

Library of Congress Cataloging-in-Publication Data
Townsend, John, 1955-
  Robberies and heists / John Townsend.
    p. cm. – (Solve it with science)
  Includes index.
  ISBN 978-1-59920-333-1 (hardcover)
  1. Robbery–Case studies–Juvenile literature. 2. Robbery investigation–Case studies–Juvenile literature. I. Title.
  HV6652.T67 2010
  363.25'9552-dc22
                                    2009002338

9 8 7 6 5 4 3 2 1

Picture credits:
Corbis: 4 (Anthony Redpath), 14 (Bettmann), 28 (moodboard), 40 (Ken Seet), 42 (PNC/Brand X).
Getty: 6 (Sean Gallup/Staff), 10 (Evening Standard/Stringer).
PA Photos: cover *right* and 12, 17 *top*, 24, 26.
Rex Features: 17 *bottom*, 18, 19, 32 (Sipa Press), 33 (Sipa Press), 34 (Allover Press Norway), 36 (Photonews Service Ltd), 37.
Science Photo Library: 7 (Mauro Fermariello), 8 (Sheila Terry), 9 (Philippe Psaila), 11 (Mauro Fermariello), 13 (Mauro Fermariello), 21 (Louise Murray), 22 (Jim Varney), 23 (Mauro Fermariello), 27 (Mauro Fermariello), 29 (Pascal Goetgheluck), 30 (Kevin Curtis), 31 (Mauro Fermariello), 35 (Philippe Plailly), 39 (Volker Steger), 41 (Mauro Fermariello), 43 (Richard Wehr/Custom Medical Stock Photo).
Shutterstock: cover *crowbar* (ajt), cover *safe* (sagasan), 5 (Gina Sanders), 15 (crystalfoto), 16 (Stephen Finn), 20 (6493866629), 25 (Maja Schon), 38 (photobeps).

Every attempt has been made to clear copyright. Should there be any inadvertent omission, please apply to the publisher for rectification.

All words in **bold** may be found in the glossary on pages 46–47.

CONTENTS

INTRODUCTION

It's a quiet day at the bank—until there's a scream. An armed robber in a ski mask runs in and shouts, "Get down on the floor!" Other robbers burst in, waving guns and demand "Hand over the money!"

Armed men rob a bank.

Scenes like this often appear in film dramas or crime TV shows. Although such robberies don't often happen, they can be hard to solve, even when they're filmed on **CCTV** cameras. The robbers usually grab the cash before running off to a waiting car, and then it's all over.

But for the police, it's just the start of a long and detailed investigation. They must search the crime scene to find every tiny detail that might lead to the robbers. It can be a difficult job, but more often than not, robbers leave behind clues. Many robbers are in prison today because they were more concerned about what they were taking away than what they were leaving behind.

4

ROBBERY

Robbery is theft with violence or the threat of violence. Although bank robbery gangs make news headlines, most robbers work alone. Some strike in dark streets, and their crime lasts less than a minute. They often use a weapon to carry out a mugging.

Whether they are an organized gang planning a major **heist** to steal money or a single robber working alone, criminals now have to worry about the latest technology used by police scientists. The science of solving robberies and heists has had major advances in recent years.

Robbers use threats and fear. Unlike some criminals, they are aggressive thieves who try to scare others to get what they want. But they often get what they don't want —a prison sentence! That's because forensic scientists (people who use science as part of a criminal investigation) are skilled at finding the smallest clues left behind after a robbery. Very often, those clues can prove who committed the crime.

A lone robber breaks into a house.

Crime scene investigators search for clues following a bank robbery in Berlin in 2007.

FINDING EVIDENCE

TV cops make it look so easy. They arrive at the crime scene, start dusting for prints, find a clue, and arrest a **suspect**! Real crime detection isn't always as fast as that. So what usually happens?

First, the crime scene is sealed off and carefully photographed. Nothing can be touched. Next, all witnesses need to provide statements and be interviewed. Meanwhile, crime scene investigators (CSIs) study every surface, search the floor, and collect tiny fragments of material for testing.

Some of the clues CSIs look for include:
- prints, such as fingerprints, shoe prints, and tire marks
- tiny particles, known as **trace evidence**, such as soil, glass, **fibers**, chemicals, gun residue, and flakes of paint
- **DNA** samples, found in blood, hair, sweat, or **saliva**

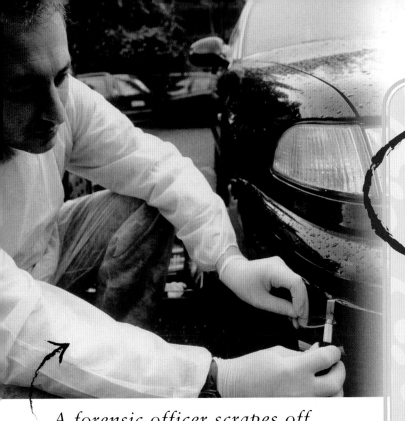

A forensic officer scrapes off some paint transferred to a vehicle from a getaway car when they collided. Comparing this paint with known paint samples can help identify the other car.

- paper, such as dropped wrappers, paper notes with messages, and handwriting clues

It can take many hours to find a clue. Items from the crime scene must be sealed in bags to prevent contamination and are then sent to scientists at the **crime lab**. It is up to them to examine tiny traces with special equipment or chemicals to see if they reveal a

EVERY CONTACT LEAVES A TRACE

More than 100 years ago, the French scientist Edmund Locard determined that when two objects touch, they transfer trace evidence. In other words, tiny particles, like specks of dust, are moved from one item to another. People leave tiny traces behind them wherever they go. This trace evidence can often be seen under a microscope. In 1910, Locard became a professor of forensic science. He set up the first police crime laboratory.

clue about the robber's identity. The packaging, labeling, and handling of evidence requires care. One mistake will make the evidence useless when any suspects go to court.

FINGERS POINT TO ROBBERS

One night in 1905, Alfred Stratton and his brother Albert broke into a shop in Deptford, London. They were looking for money, but the owner heard them. The robbers attacked, there was a struggle, and soon both the shopkeeper and his wife lay dying. The brothers grabbed the cash and ran. The next day, police found a thumbprint on an empty cash box in the shop.

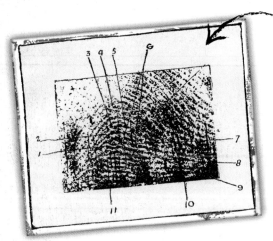

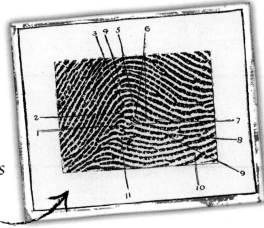

The thumbprint found on the cash box (left) matched Albert Stratton's (right). On this evidence, the brothers were found guilty.

The police arrested the Stratton brothers as suspects. They took their thumbprints and found that Albert's matched the one on the cash box. This case made **legal** history because it was the first time a **jury** accepted a print as proof. The brothers were **convicted** of murder and hanged.

FINGERPRINTS

Whenever you touch something, you leave a smear of grease, dust, or sweat behind. Human skin is full of tiny lines and marks. The image of the **unique** pattern on your fingers stays on most things you touch. It proves you were there.

It's the same with hands, knees, feet, lips, and even tongue prints. In 1892, British scientist Francis Galton wrote a book about fingerprints and how they could solve crimes.

FINGERPRINT DESIGNS

The patterns on our fingertips have different designs.

• **Arches are formed by ridges running across the print. About 5 percent of people have this print.**

• **Whorls may form a complete oval, often in a spiral pattern. About 30 percent of people have this pattern.**

• **Loops have a stronger curve than arches. About 60 percent of fingerprints have loops.**

• **Some people have a mixture of these patterns.**

THOMAS JENNINGS

In 1910, Thomas Jennings was the first American robber to be convicted on the evidence of fingerprints. When he broke into a home in Chicago, Illinois, and shot the owner, he left four clear prints in wet paint. Fingerprint experts convinced the jury that this proved Jennings was the killer. He was sentenced to death. From then on, fingerprints were used as evidence throughout the United States.

A forensic scientist uses powder to reveal fingerprints on a pane of glass at a crime scene.

9

THE GREAT TRAIN ROBBERY

Fingerprints helped to convict a gang that carried out one of the biggest robberies in England. On an August night in 1963, a gang robbed a train carrying sacks of money worth about $60 million today.

The robbers stopped the train by changing a signal from green to red and then climbed on board. They clubbed the driver, who was badly injured. While threatening the staff on the train, 15 robbers wearing ski masks and helmets got to work unloading 120 money sacks. Within 30 minutes, the gang had loaded a truck and driven off to their hideout—a vacant farm.

This is the scene of the Great Train Robbery in August 1963. The train stopped on a bridge above a country road where the gang members waited.

A forensic officer uses a sticky plastic strip to lift a fingerprint from a cup. It can then be taken to the crime lab for analysis.

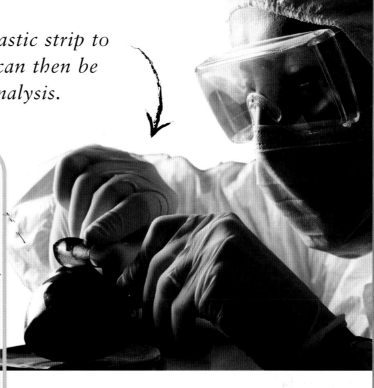

FINDING, LIFTING, AND MATCHING FINGERPRINTS

By dusting surfaces with a fine powder, fingerprint experts are able to find prints that normally would be invisible. They use tape or a plastic strip to "lift" the print so it can be taken to the crime lab. The forensic team then photographs and enlarges it for careful study.

The print can be compared with those of known criminals whose fingerprints are already on record or compared with the prints of a suspect. Even if a suspect swears he was miles away from the robbery, if his fingerprints are at the crime scene, he's **guilty!**

PRINTS EVERYWHERE

For a few days, the robbers stayed in their hideout while the robbery made world news. They left the farm shortly before the police arrived. Forensic scientists soon got to work in the deserted hideout and found fingerprints everywhere. Windows, plates, beverage cans, and a board game were covered in prints.

This and other evidence helped the police find most of the robbers. In just over six months, 12 of the 15 robbers were given prison sentences totaling over 300 years.

THE BLACK PANTHER

One of Britain's most wanted robbers in the 1970s was a man who worked alone. After breaking into a number of houses in Yorkshire, UK, he began to travel further afield, robbing small post offices using a gun. Because he always wore a dark ski mask during his attacks, the robber became known as the Black Panther. Before long, he shot and killed those he robbed.

Donald Neilson, the Black Panther

DARK CLUE

In 1974, the Black Panther held up a post office in the West Midlands. The postmaster put up a fight and sprayed **ammonia** in the robber's face. Screaming in pain, the Black Panther shot and killed the postmaster before running off.

When forensic scientists arrived at the crime scene, they found splashes of dark blue dye on the post office floor. The ammonia had made some of the dye leak out of the ski mask and scientists were soon able to **identify** the dye.

THE ARREST

A year later, a police officer stopped Donald Neilson for a minor offense. When they searched Neilson's home, the police found a dark blue ski mask. The forensic scientists examined it and found that the dark blue dye was **identical** to the sample found on the floor of the post office the robber had struck.

Not only was Neilson the Black Panther robber, but he was also a cruel killer who had kidnapped a girl. The evidence was in his attic. He confessed to several robberies and murders. He was sentenced to life in prison.

DYE IN THE LAB

By using chemicals and special machines that shine light through fabric, scientists can tell a lot from dyes used in clothes. In many ways, dyes are like fingerprints as no two are exactly the same. An instrument called a **spectrometer** uses rays of light to measure details in the dye. This enables the crime lab to determine if a sample of dye came from a thread in an item of clothing.

A forensic scientist uses a mass spectrometer. This equipment is used to analyze substances such as dyes to discover their chemical composition.

CAUGHT BY THE JEANS

Armed robbers escaped from a bank in Spokane, Washington, in 1996 with thousands of dollars. The gang had already struck many times in this area, and this robbery was like the others. The robbers knew they were filmed, but they didn't care as they always wore masks to conceal their identities. The fact that a CCTV camera showed the legs of one robber in close-up would not have worried them. What can you possibly learn from a pair of jeans?

UNIQUE

All pairs of jeans are slightly different. The fabric becomes worn, marked, and bunched in different ways, making tiny white bands—like a unique bar code. Creases, bumps, holes, and faded dye can tell scientists a lot.

A bank robbery in New York City in 1974 is recorded on the bank's CCTV camera. Unlike the Spokane robbers, these men didn't bother with masks.

14

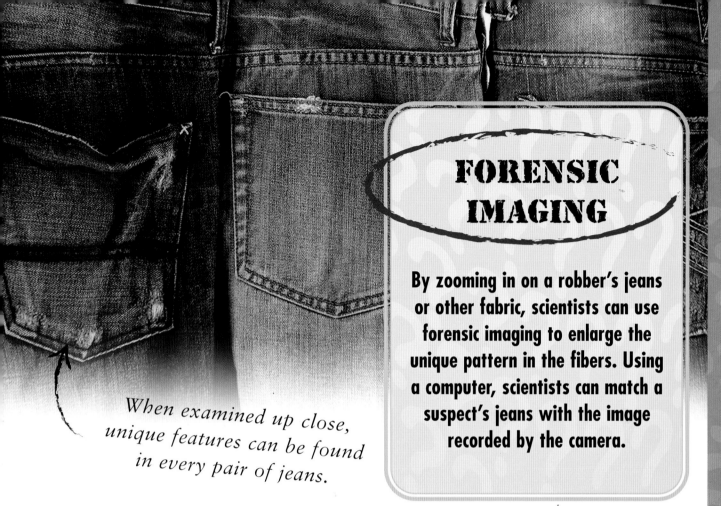

When examined up close, unique features can be found in every pair of jeans.

FORENSIC IMAGING

By zooming in on a robber's jeans or other fabric, scientists can use forensic imaging to enlarge the unique pattern in the fibers. Using a computer, scientists can match a suspect's jeans with the image recorded by the camera.

VIDEO EVIDENCE

FBI forensic scientists examined a video from the Spokane bank robbery. One of the robbers had stood still long enough for the camera to record part of his jeans in very good detail. A close-up image of a worn patch clearly showed all the fibers in the denim fabric.

The police had several suspects for the robbery. One of them wore a pair of jeans with more than 24 features that matched the "bar code" of the jeans on the video. The suspect was arrested on this evidence and went to court.

PROOF

At the trial, the suspect's **defense** team said the jeans didn't prove anything because all jeans looked the same. They even showed 34 similar pairs in court. But the FBI scientists proved they could distinguish the suspect's jeans from every other pair. The robber was convicted—all because of his jeans.

HEIST OF THE MILLENNIUM

At the start of the year 2000, big events were underway to mark the new millennium. One of them was top secret. It was a plan by a gang to rob the Millennium Dome in London. It would be the biggest robbery on record. At least, that was the plan—but police forensic scientists were already at work.

THE RAID ON THE DOME DIAMOND

Britain's capital city London had something special to mark the year 2000. The Millennium Dome by the River Thames was full of displays for visitors to see. One display was the Millennium Star— an egg-sized diamond worth $566.5 million at that time. But a gang of robbers wanted it and had been planning for months to steal it.

The Millennium Dome in London

SMASHED AND ALMOST GRABBED

On November 7, 2000, the robbers drove a bulldozer at high speed through the Millennium Dome's outer fence. At 9:30 A.M., the bulldozer smashed into the dome. Once inside, the gang attacked the display case with sledgehammers, nail guns, and gas bombs. A boat awaited them on the river to speed away with the diamond. But things didn't go as planned.

The police were ready and waiting. The forensic team had been at work and were prepared. The diamond had been secretly replaced with a fake. The police dressed as cleaners and had hidden guns. Although the police were armed, not a shot was fired. They shouted, "Freeze!" and the gang fell to the ground. More than 100 police officers were ready. Only 64 visitors were in the dome at the time. Luckily, no one was hurt in the biggest robbery that never was.

A CCTV image shows a robber smashing the glass case containing the Millennium Star. The diamond in this case was actually a fake.

The Millennium Star

"This would have been the largest robbery in the world."
John Shatford, Metropolitan Police

"I was just inches away from payday. It would have been a blinding Christmas!"
Bob Adams, robber

HOW DID FORENSIC SCIENCE PREVENT THE DOME ROBBERY?

When a CSI team found saliva on a pair of rubber gloves in a van used in a robbery in Kent, they did some tests in the lab. They extracted DNA from the saliva and found that this matched the DNA of Lee Wenham, a known robber.

This is the bulldozer used in the attempted robbery.

THE SCIENCE OF DNA

DNA stands for deoxyribonucleic acid. It is like a special code locked in your **genes**. DNA holds all the instructions that make you unique. Hair, skin cells, blood, body fluids, and body tissue all contain DNA. If any of these substances are found at a crime scene, they can be used to prove that a particular person was there. They also can prove someone is **innocent**.

Rather than arrest Wenham immediately, the police decided to watch him closely. They felt sure he was planning another robbery, so they followed him. They watched him as he went around the Millennium Dome, taking a special interest in the Millennium Star diamond. The police now knew where the next robbery would be—but they didn't know when.

For weeks, the police kept a close lookout, hoping to catch the gang redhanded. That's just what happened. The robbers had planned to destroy all forensic evidence. The bulldozer and speedboat contained full cans of gasoline so they could set fire to them when they fled. But they didn't get the chance, as all the men were arrested.

Lee Wenham was jailed for nine years for his part in the heist.

PRISON
In 2002, the five members of the gang went to court. The sixth member had died in 2001. The boat driver was sentenced to prison for five years for plotting to steal. The other men were found guilty of attempted robbery and received a total of 66 years in prison.

SHOE CLUE

In 2000, an armed robber was on his way to rob a bank in Australia and didn't look where he was walking. He stepped into something a dog had left behind! Despite the mess on his shoe, 26-year-old Jacob Smith ran into the Gold Coast bank. He hid his face by wrapping a sheet around his head. But the mess on his shoe left a print on the floor.

Watch your step! Luckily for the police, Jacob Smith didn't watch his.

Forensic scientists had the smelly job of examining the shoe prints left in the bank. "It's the first time I've ever got a pattern left by dog poop," said the forensic science officer. "It could have been one of a thousand or ten thousand shoes, but because the poop was there it was creating a great big feature that allowed us to go to a positive identification."

WHIFF OF GUILT

When the suspect's shoe was examined by the police, they were able to match it to the pattern from the crime scene. Also, the dog waste in the tread matched the sample they found at the bank! Their investigation showed how the robber had stepped in several clumps of dog waste before the robbery. He should have watched his step. He was sent to prison for 10 years for robbery—a sentence not to be sniffed at!

SHOE SCIENCE

Messy shoes and the material from the prints they leave behind can give forensic scientists a great deal of information. Mud on a shoe can show exactly where the wearer has been because the type of soil and the tiny pollen grains in it can be matched to a particular area—sometimes revealing exactly where a suspect has walked.

A forensic scientist analyzes material found in the tread of a shoe.

SHOE PRINT SCIENCE

Police rushed to the Standard Federal Bank in Fort Wayne, Indiana, in 2001. The bank's alarm had gone off in the night. As they searched, the police saw a masked man run from the back door. He vanished into the darkness. A passerby reported seeing someone behaving strangely in the shadows. The police found the man and arrested him. They thought he looked like the suspect who had run from the bank, but how could they be sure?

PRINTS IN THE MUD

The police forensic team studied shoe prints in the mud outside the back door of the bank. They made molds of them so they could study them in the lab. Then they compared the pattern of the prints with those on the suspect's shoes. They were a direct match.

A forensics officer holds a plaster cast of a shoe print discovered at the scene of a crime. The cast can be compared to suspects' footwear to find a match.

A forensic scientist analyzes a print made from a suspect's shoe. This can be compared with shoe prints found at a crime scene.

SHOE PROOF

A clear shoe print can be left at a crime scene in mud, sand, or snow. Forensic scientists photograph the print, then make a cast. Making a cast in snow has to be done very carefully because it can be easily damaged. Scientists use liquid sulfur, which quickly cools as it touches the snow and hardens to catch the exact impression. At the lab, a computer **analyzes** every detail of the print. Each shoe print is as unique as a fingerprint. Soles of shoes become worn or marked by sharp objects. Cuts, scratches, or tiny stones wedged in the tread all leave telltale marks. The police can examine a suspect's shoes to find a match.

Anthony Allen went on trial. His defense was that shoe print evidence couldn't prove anything as his shoes wouldn't have been the only ones to match the prints found at the crime scene. Allen failed to convince the court, which decided shoe prints make good evidence.

GLASS

A gang of violent armed robbers from Leeds, UK, raided supermarkets, banks, and post offices across Yorkshire during 2000 and 2001. They carried out over 30 robberies, using pickax handles, guns, baseball bats, and ammonia spray. A victim lost the sight in one eye after being sprayed in the face with ammonia. In total, the gang stole well over $1.5 million in cash.

EVIDENCE

The police had a number of suspects in mind, but they needed to find firm proof to link the suspects to the robberies. They finally arrested eight men between the ages of 18 and 26. Forensic scientists were able to prove the suspects had been involved in the robberies by examining the men's clothes. There were three main pieces of evidence.

- One of the cash boxes they stole let off smoke and special security dye when it was broken open. The same dye was on the suspects' clothes and on the cash in their possession.

This CCTV image shows a young robber brandishing a gun in a shop in Liverpool, UK, in 2001.

- Scientists found rare nylon fibers at the crime scenes. These matched the fibers in some of the suspects' gloves.
- Tiny pieces of smashed glass from the crime scenes were found on the suspects' tools and their shoes.

Police scientists had enough evidence to convict seven of the suspects in court in 2003. The robbers were each given long prison sentences.

Light rays pass at varying speeds through glass. These different speeds can be compared to find a match.

ANALYZING GLASS

Scientists can tell if tiny glass fragments found on clothes match those at a crime scene. Under a microscope, all kinds of clues are visible. You may think all glass is the same, but tests can show whether or not two fragments of glass are from the same pane. A chemical test can show if both pieces of glass are made in exactly the same way. Another test measures beams of light reflecting from the glass samples. If the measurements match, the samples are from the same pane of glass.

FIBERS

In June 2001, two South London, UK robbers broke into an apartment belonging to 54-year-old Michael Reaney. In the course of the robbery, Reaney confronted them and the robbers killed him.

The police found a clue to the robbers' identities when they checked recent calls made on Reaney's phone. One was to Selina Hall, the girlfriend of Francis Carbon, a suspect in several recent holdups in the area. Carbon and his friend, Andrew Docherty, were put under police **surveillance**. They were arrested while trying to rob a liquor store. The police searched their homes.

A MASS OF EVIDENCE

Following the search, a large number of items were taken for testing. Forensic scientists found that fibers on a pair of gloves at Carbon's home matched the fibers found on the tape that had been used on Reaney's face.

Francis Carbon

FIBER ANALYSIS

When looking for a match between two fibers, forensic scientists carry out a number of tests. First, they use a **comparison microscope** to compare the color and appearance of the fibers. If they appear to match, the comparison is repeated under **infrared** or **ultraviolet** light. For example, an **infrared spectrometry** test measures the amount of infrared light that is absorbed when it passes through a fiber. This is recorded in a series of peaks and troughs, which together form the fiber's unique signature. If the signatures of the two fibers are identical, the fibers match.

Forensic tests on the items found in the search revealed Carbon and Docherty's links to several other crimes. Blood traces were found on a roll of black tape, a handgun, a crash helmet, and athletic shoes. Through DNA tests, forensic scientists were able to match these traces to the blood of some of the victims of recent liquor store robberies.

SENTENCE

Carbon and Docherty were convicted of a series of crimes. Carbon was sentenced to 11 years in jail and Docherty was sentenced to 15 years.

A magnified photo of fibers found at a crime scene. The fibers can be compared to fiber samples taken from a suspect to try to find a match.

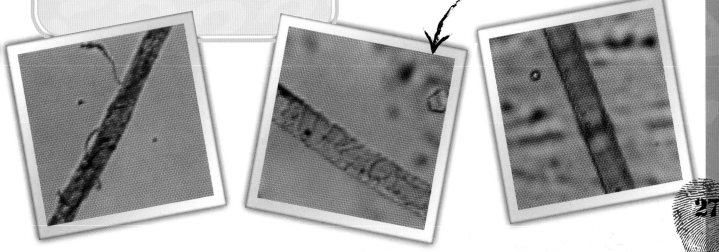

HAIR

In the early hours of December 7, 2002, thieves climbed a ladder up to a window at the back of the Van Gogh Museum in Amsterdam. They used a large cloth to protect their hands as they smashed through the glass to get into the building full of paintings.

The thieves grabbed two paintings by the Dutch artist Vincent van Gogh, valued at $3 million, before climbing back out of the window. They slid down a rope to the ground, then ran off with the paintings. The alarm went off, but police couldn't get to the museum in time to catch the thieves.

CLUES

Forensic scientists searched for clues. They found a lot of evidence, including the cloth, ladder, and rope used by the thieves in the raid. They took the cloth and bits of glass from the broken window for analysis. Police studied video tapes recorded by CCTV cameras.

However, the vital clues came from the caps left by the thieves. Inside the headwear, forensic scientists found dandruff (dead skin cells) and hair. Both of these contain DNA.

Robbers often leave clues in the form of hair or fibers on smashed glass.

CAUGHT

A year after the robbery, the police arrested two suspects. Although the men denied stealing the paintings, their DNA matched the samples from the caps found at the crime scene. Both men were sent to prison, but the paintings have yet to be found.

A forensic scientist examines bands of DNA extracted from a hair root. The bands glow pink under ultraviolet light.

DNA FROM HAIR

Shafts of hair are mostly made up of dead cells, which are not a good source of DNA. However, the root, or bulb, at the base of the hair shaft is made of living cells and contains healthy DNA. The root lies next to the **follicle**, a narrow tube in the skin from which hair grows. In order to extract DNA from hair, scientists need to find a complete strand, including the root.

BLOOD

In 2003, a gang of armed robbers raided a chain of restaurants and businesses in Kentucky. The robbers were such show-offs they even phoned their victims beforehand to warn them they were about to be robbed! The gang mainly attacked restaurants with poor CCTV equipment and weren't often caught on video. Sometimes, they injured people by tying them up, gagging, and even stabbing them.

KNIFE WOUND

After as many as 100 robberies, one of the gang members cut himself while waving a knife. He ran away, but the police gathered the blood at the scene and forensic scientists examined it. They checked DNA records and soon had a perfect match with Tommy Jerome Hardin, a known criminal.

Hardin and his gang were soon arrested and charged with armed robbery. Although he escaped, Hardin was caught again and put behind bars where he will be kept secure for a long time.

A forensic officer holds a bloodstained knife found at a crime scene.

Even if clothes have been washed, scientists can still find traces of blood in the fabric. A chemical called **luminol** will make any blood glow under ultraviolet light. The pattern and shape of blood splashes at a crime scene can also be important. Forensic scientists can use this evidence to piece together what happened during the course of the crime.

THE SECRETS OF BLOOD

In 1901, scientist Karl Landsteiner developed a system of classifying blood into four main groups. They are called A, B, AB, and O. Types A and O are the most common blood groups in humans. AB is the most rare.

Gradually, blood identification grew more precise. By 1950, scientists could even tell if a blood sample came from a male or female. Today, a tiny speck of blood can be matched to a particular person.

A forensic scientist examines a piece of bloodstained clothing.

31

THE SCREAM

In August 2004, one of the most famous paintings in the world was stolen in broad daylight in a violent raid. Robbers burst into an art museum in Oslo, Norway, and pointed a gun at one of the staff. Stunned tourists watched helplessly as the hooded gang grabbed two famous paintings, *The Scream* and *Madonna*, by Norwegian artist Edvard Munch. The robbers ran from the museum to a waiting getaway car.

The Scream had been on display at the Munch Museum in Oslo. Edvard Munch (1863–1944) had produced several versions of the painting. Art experts valued the stolen version at $100 million. It was not the first time *The Scream* had been stolen by thieves. Another version had been stolen in 1994 and found three months later.

ESCAPE

Two robbers were filmed running from the museum to a waiting car. They dropped one of the paintings twice in their dash to the car. As they drove off, they threw the frames out of the window, maybe fearing a tracking device had been implanted in the wood. The police later found the empty frames nearby.

The Munch Museum robbers head for the getaway car.

32

A forensic officer examines the getaway car, a black Audi, that the robbers abandoned in Oslo.

DNA EVIDENCE

The robbers made sure they covered their tracks by wiping their fingerprints from the frames and setting off a fire extinguisher in the abandoned getaway car. They thought this would destroy all DNA evidence. However, some DNA remained that forensic scientists described as "useful biological trace evidence."

CLUES IN THE GETAWAY CAR

Forensic scientists are often able to find DNA evidence in cars even after criminals have tried to get rid of all traces. Robbers have been caught from:

• saliva in chewing gum or on cigarette ends

• lip prints and saliva left on drink cans

• fingernail shreds—nervous robbers sometimes bite their nails as they drive off

• hairs on the headrest

ARRESTS

A year after the theft of *The Scream*, the police arrested four suspects. By early 2006, two more men were arrested and all six men went on trial, even though the police still hadn't found the stolen paintings. The Oslo government offered a reward of $320 million for any information that could lead to the recovery of the paintings.

The court case was reported around the world. Would there be enough proof to convict the men and would they say where the paintings were hidden?

GUILTY

The police were able to prove in court that the suspects were guilty of the robbery. The evidence came from the DNA found in the getaway car and from **digital** forensics. That meant evidence obtained from telephone records and from tapping 60,000 calls. This was enough evidence to convict the men.

In May 2006, three of the robbers were sentenced to prison for between four and eight years.

Police display the recovered Munch masterpiece The Scream *at a press conference.*

DIGITAL FINGERPRINTS

The fingerprints of convicted criminals are now recorded digitally by machine. At one time, their prints were made with ink and stored in paper files. Now fingerprints are read by machine and stored electronically, along with their DNA profile. If the criminal leaves prison and commits another robbery, any evidence left at the crime scene will be quickly identified by computer.

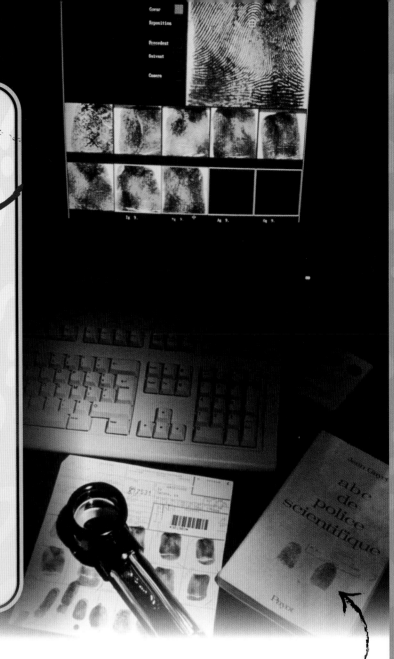

Three months later, newspapers reported that the Edvard Munch masterpieces, *The Scream* and *Madonna*, had been recovered and returned.

After being repaired, the famous paintings were put back on display in 2008. Now the museum has far better security!

In a computerized fingerprint system, the digitizer (bottom) converts paper copies of criminals' fingerprints into digital form. Fingerprints are enlarged and displayed side by side on the computer screen for detailed analysis.

NEW HEIST OF THE MILLENNIUM

On the night of February 21, 2006, an armed gang carried out Britain's biggest robbery. The gang stole more than $92 million in cash from a security depot in Kent.

A CCTV image of the robbers loading up the truck before making their escape.

DISGUISED AS POLICE

The raid began when robbers kidnapped the depot's manager at gunpoint, along with his wife and eight-year-old son. Because the robbers were **disguised** as police, they were able to pass through tight security before bursting into the depot. Now wearing masks, the robbers tied up 15 workers and forced the manager to load sacks of money into a truck. They then sped away with the money.

An hour passed before one of the staff was able to free himself and raise the alarm. The manager's wife and son were released unhurt. The police soon found the robbers' abandoned truck. Forensic scientists immediately went to work on the truck and at the suspects' homes.

FORENSIC SCIENCE AT HOME

Many suspects are arrested because of evidence found at their homes. Forensic teams often look for various types of clues in people's houses. That can mean taking material back to the crime lab for detailed tests. Information can be gathered from firearms, clothing, computers, cell phones, and even money.

FORENSIC CLUES

At the home of suspect Lea Rusha, police found a plan of the security depot with his fingerprints on it. His DNA was found on a ski mask in the abandoned truck. The DNA of another suspect, Roger Coutts, was found on 9 of the 11 cable ties used to tie up the employees. Jetmir Bucpapa, another suspect, was also linked to the crime through his DNA found on a suitcase containing money stolen in the raid.

SENTENCE

In 2008, the robbers went on trial. The judge said they were "ruthless bandits" and sentenced five of the men to a total of over 70 years in prison.

Lea Rusha was one of the fake policemen who kidnapped the depot manager and his family.

FACE PRINTS

When a robber snatched handfuls of dollar bills from a service station in Rhode Island, in 2007, he had no idea that new technology would catch him. Witnesses described him as a white male between 35 and 60 years old with gray hair. That wasn't much for the police to go on, but they hoped to find more clues in a video recording of the robbery from the station's CCTV system.

The police used a new video forensic system. This uses computer software combined with advanced digital technology to sharpen video images frame by frame. The Rhode Island police were able to obtain very clear images of the robber as well as the license plate of his car.

Clear photos of the robber were put on Rhode Island's Most Wanted Web site and run on the nightly television news. A few days after the

Fuzzy CCTV images from a security camera can now be improved to make identification of criminals easier.

38

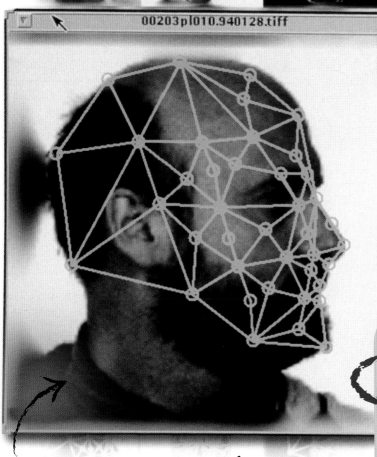

00203pl010.940128.tiff

A computer creates a face print from a picture of a man's head. Each person's face print is unique.

robbery, the police received a call informing them of a likely suspect. When they arrived at the suspect's house, police found the getaway car. Police scientists then took a photograph of the suspect's face and used face technology to match it exactly to the video image from the crime.

On the strength of this evidence, the man was convicted of robbing the service station.

READING FACES

A digital photo of a suspect's face is like a face print. Police compare it with a video image from the crime scene using face recognition software. This analyzes the spaces and angles between 80 key points on a person's face. Data from only 14 to 20 such points is enough to make a unique face print that can then be matched to a **database** of face prints from pictures of wanted criminals. Our faces, like our fingerprints and our DNA, are like no one else's in the world.

SALIVA

Robbers' mouths give them away—not from what they say, but from their spit! In 2007, a robber ran into a crowded bank in Santa Clara, California, and fired a bullet into the ceiling above terrified customers. This was the third time he had robbed the same bank, yet he was sure no one would recognize him as he wore a mask.

UNMASKED

The robber, 28-year-old Froilan Alix Roldan, fled the bank. On his way out, he dropped his mask. Scientists found a speck of saliva on the mask and it matched Roldan's DNA. On his arrest Roldan said to police, "You got me from the mask." He was dead right!

CAUGHT

In 2008, two 16-year-old girls chased a robber in Burnley, UK, after he stole $300 from a woman at a bank machine. The girls were unable to catch him, but they saw him drop a cigarette. Police scientists took the cigarette for testing. DNA extracted from the saliva found on the cigarette turned out to be a direct match to a known robber. Within days of the robbery, the man was arrested and charged. He pleaded guilty and was sentenced to 12 months in prison.

Saliva traces left in a discarded mask can provide vital evidence for forensic scientists.

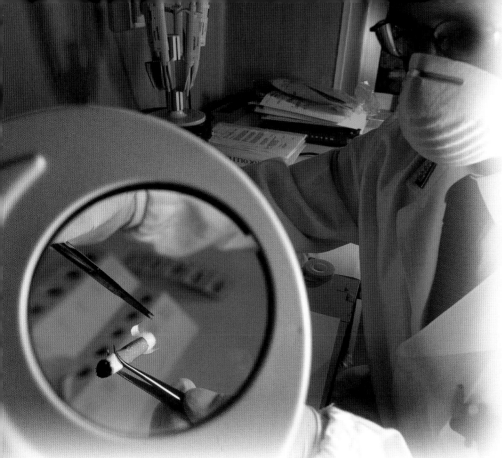

A forensic scientist peels off the filter paper of a cigarette butt found at a crime scene. DNA extracted from saliva traces on the filter paper can link a suspect to the crime.

CARJACKING GANG

In early 2002, a seven-man gang of violent robbers carried out a series of car thefts in North London. Their luck ran out on March 26 when they broke into a house and demanded the keys to the BMW in the driveway. While the owner went to get the keys, one gang member, Leon Willoughby, threw a half-eaten kebab out of the window. This was a mistake. DNA in the saliva on the kebab was traced to Willoughby. The gang was arrested, convicted, and sentenced to between 9 and 14 years in prison.

SPITTING IMAGE

Saliva is a good source of DNA. Therefore it is very useful as a means of identifying criminals. It is easier to extract than blood, and even very small samples can yield clues. Scientists can retrieve enough saliva from a licked postage stamp to identify the person who licked it.

SWEAT

In 2008, a man robbed a bank in Centralia, Washington, and left behind a sweaty clue. Running from the bank, he fled down an alley. Hot and sweaty, he removed the coat and knit cap he had worn so that the CCTV image would not be able to identify him by the clothes. Two women saw him throw the items into a trash bin. Forensic scientists began looking for clues on these clothes.

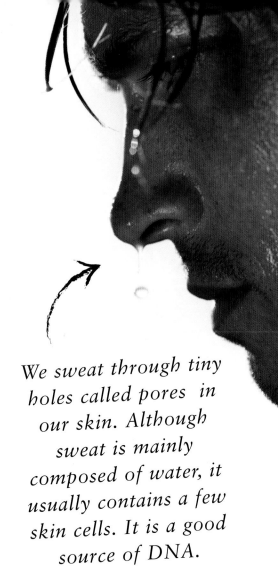

We sweat through tiny holes called pores in our skin. Although sweat is mainly composed of water, it usually contains a few skin cells. It is a good source of DNA.

HOT WORK

"The coat and the hat were the key to solving this," said Detective Carl Buster of the Centralia Police. DNA testing came up with a match. Michael Anduiza was also convicted of robbing four banks in Seattle. The sweat in the hat and coat provided the DNA forensic scientists needed!

SWEATY FACE

Three armed robbers burst into a jewelery shop in Cambridge, UK, in July 2006. They escaped with watches worth about $260,000. The following week, they robbed a jeweler in Norwich. The gang leader, Kulder Ojaaar, held a gun to the throat of a shop assistant, but her colleagues attacked the robbers who fled empty-handed.

When the police arrived, they took swabs from the shop assistant's face to obtain traces of Ojaaar's sweat. The police knew the gang was from Estonia, and they contacted police there. The Estonian police were able to identify Ojaaar from their DNA database. Ojaaar admitted the attempted robbery in Norwich and the robbery in Cambridge. He was jailed for 11 years.

MAKING THEM SWEAT

DNA can be extracted from any part of the human body that contains cells. Sweat does not contain cells, but it usually contains skin cells that have been shed. This is helpful for crime scene investigators because nervous robbers are likely to perspire. Traces of their sweat are frequently found at crime scenes. For example, steering wheels on stolen cars, dropped gloves, pairs of glasses, and masks have all yielded sweat traces.

This highly magnified view of the back of a hand shows sweat droplets (blue) emerging from the sweat glands in the skin.

TIME LINE

1686	Marcello Malpighi notes the differences between fingerprints.
1835	Henry Goddard of Britain's Scotland Yard is the first to prove a bullet was fired from a particular gun.
1877	Thomas Taylor believes fingerprints might help to identify criminals.
1892	Juan Vucetich develops the first fingerprint pattern system.
1901	Karl Landsteiner discovers human blood groups.
1903	The New York State Prison system begins the first use in the United States of fingerprints for criminal identification.
1905	Theodore Roosevelt establishes the Federal Bureau of Investigation (FBI).
1910	Edmond Locard sets up the first police crime laboratory in France.
1910	Victor Balthazard publishes the first detailed study of hair for criminal identification.
1913	Victor Balthazard publishes the first article on bullet identification.
1916	Albert Schneider invents a vacuum device to collect trace evidence.
1932	The FBI crime laboratory is created.
1941	Murray Hill begins to study voiceprint identification.
1950	Max Frei-Sutzer develops a method of collecting trace evidence by lifting evidence with tape.
1959	U.S. police officer Hugh MacDonald develops Identikit.

1970	British inventor Jacques Penry develops Photo-fit, which uses photographed features.
1978	The first facial identification system is developed by the Computer-Aided Design Center in Cambridge, UK. It is later developed into E-fit.
1978	Laser technology is introduced to detect fingerprints.
1984	The first automatic fingerprint recognition system is installed at Scotland Yard.
1986	DNA typing is first used to solve a crime.
1990s	The National Integrated Ballistic Identification Network (NIBIN), a national database for identifying bullets and guns, is developed in the United States.
1991	Canada develops the first Integrated Ballistics Imaging System (IBIS). It compares the different marks on bullets and shells.
1995	The world's first criminal intelligence DNA database is launched in the UK.
1998	U.S. scientists create the Combined DNA Index System. This allows crime laboratories across the United States to compare DNA samples with a national database.
2006	New technology allowing fingerprint images to be compressed and transmitted via mobile phones is approved for use by the British police.
2008	Dr. John Bond of Northamptonshire Police develops a technique for recovering fingerprints from bullets after they have been fired.
2008	In Milan, Italy, masked thieves drill a tunnel and break into a jewelery showroom. They make off with gold, diamonds, and rubies in a daring daylight heist.

GLOSSARY

ammonia
A strong-smelling gas or liquid that harms the eyes.

analyze
Study and examine details very closely.

CCTV
Closed-circuit television.

comparison microscope
A microscope that shows two things at the same time so that they can be compared.

convict
Find or prove guilty.

crime lab
A laboratory where police scientists study evidence from crime scenes.

database
A collection of information that is held on a computer.

defense
An argument in support of something in a court of law.

digital
Processing, storing, transmitting, or displaying data in the form of numerical digits, as in a digital computer.

disguised
Changed in appearance to hide the real identity.

DNA
A chemical molecule that carries genetic information; everyone's DNA is slightly different, and it can be used to identify a particular individual.

FBI
The crime-fighting Federal Bureau of Investigation in the United States.

fiber
Tiny thread.

follicle
A small cavity in the skin. It contains the cells that produce hair.

gene
The set of genetic instructions contained in a person's body cells.

guilty
Having done wrong or being responsible for a crime.

heist
A large-scale and well-organized robbery.

identical
Exactly alike.

identify
Determine who or what someone or something is.

infrared
Radiation (energy waves) with wavelengths longer than visible light but shorter than radio waves.

infrared spectrometry
A method used to measure how much infrared light is absorbed when passing through a transparent substance. This measurement, known as a signature, can be compared to the signatures of other known substances to identify the unknown substance.

innocent
Not guilty of a crime.

jury
A group of citizens who hear a court case and then decide if a defendant is guilty or not.

legal
To do with the law.

luminol
A chemical used to show blood spots.

saliva
Moisture produced in the mouth.

spectrometer
An instrument that spreads particles into an ordered sequence.

surveillance
Continual observation of a person or group suspected of doing something illegal.

suspect
A person thought to be guilty of a crime.

trace evidence
Small pieces of evidence found at a crime scene, such as hair, fiber, grass, glass, soil, blood spots, and skin.

ultraviolet
Radiation (energy waves) with wavelengths shorter than visible light but longer than x-rays. Ultraviolet light is a purple light that makes some material glow in the dark.

unique
Only one of its kind.

FURTHER INFORMATION

BOOKS
CSI Expert!: Forensic Science for Kids by Karen K. Shulz (Prufrock Press, 2008)

Forensic Files: Investigating Thefts & Heists by Alex Woolf (Harcourt Education, 2004)

Forensic Science by Chris Cooper (DK Publishing, 2008)

Hair, Clothing, and Tire Track Evidence: Crime-Solving Science Experiments by Kenneth G. Rainis (Enslow Publishers, 2006)

True Crime: Cops and Robbers by John Townsend (Harcourt Education, 2006)

WEB SITES
www.fbi.gov/kids/6th12th/6th12th.htm
How the FBI investigates crimes.

www.howstuffworks.com/csi5.htm
All about the world of CSI.

library.thinkquest.org/04oct/00206/tte_every_criminal_leaves_a_trace.htm
Information about the work of forensic scientists.

INDEX